W9-AKB-764

Blue Banner Biography

Corbin Bleu

Mary Boone

Mitchell Lane
PUBLISHERS

P.O. Box 196
Hockessin, Delaware 19707
Visit us on the web: www.mitchelllane.com
Comments? email us: mitchelllane@mitchelllane.com

Mitchell Lane PUBLISHERS

Copyright © 2009 by Mitchell Lane Publishers. All rights reserved. No part of this book may be reproduced without written permission from the publisher. Printed and bound in the United States of America.

Printing   1   2   3   4   5   6   7   8   9

Blue Banner Biographies

Akon	Alan Jackson	Alicia Keys
Allen Iverson	Ashanti	Ashlee Simpson
Ashton Kutcher	Avril Lavigne	Bernie Mac
Beyoncé	Bow Wow	Brett Favre
Britney Spears	Carrie Underwood	Chris Brown
Chris Daughtry	Christina Aguilera	Christopher Paul Curtis
Ciara	Clay Aiken	Condoleezza Rice
Corbin Bleu	Daniel Radcliffe	David Ortiz
Derek Jeter	Eminem	Eve
Fergie (Stacy Ferguson)	50 Cent	Gwen Stefani
Ice Cube	Jamie Foxx	Ja Rule
Jay-Z	Jennifer Lopez	Jessica Simpson
J. K. Rowling	Johnny Depp	JoJo
Justin Berfield	Justin Timberlake	Kanye West
Kate Hudson	Keith Urban	Kelly Clarkson
Kenny Chesney	Lance Armstrong	Lindsay Lohan
Mariah Carey	Mario	Mary J. Blige
Mary-Kate and Ashley Olsen	Michael Jackson	Miguel Tejada
Missy Elliott	Nancy Pelosi	Nelly
Orlando Bloom	P. Diddy	Paris Hilton
Peyton Manning	Queen Latifah	Rihanna
Ron Howard	Rudy Giuliani	Sally Field
Sean Kingston	Selena	Shakira
Shirley Temple	Soulja Boy Tell 'Em	Taylor Swift
Timbaland	Tim McGraw	Toby Keith
Usher	Vanessa Anne Hudgens	Zac Efron

Library of Congress Cataloging-in-Publication Data
Boone, Mary.
  Corbin Bleu / By Mary Boone.
      p. cm. — (Blue banner biographies)
  Includes bibliographical references, discography, filmography and index.
  ISBN 978-1-58415-674-1 (library bound)
  1. Bleu, Corbin, 1989– —Juvenile literature. 2. Actors—United States—Biography—Juvenile literature. I. Title.
  PN2287.B457B66 2009
  791.4302'8092—dc22
  [B]
                                                                                              2008008056

ABOUT THE AUTHOR: Mary Boone has written over a dozen books for young adults, including biographies about Hilary Duff, Lindsay Lohan, and Raven for Mitchell Lane Publishers. She also has written for magazines including *People, Teen People, Mary-Kate and Ashley,* and *Entertainment Weekly.* Boone lives in Tacoma, Washington. When she's not writing she enjoys running, swimming, and being outdoors with her husband, Mitch, and their two children, Eve and Eli.

PUBLISHER'S NOTE: The following story has been thoroughly researched, and to the best of our knowledge represents a true story. While every possible effort has been made to ensure accuracy, the publisher will not assume liability for damages caused by inaccuracies in the data, and makes no warranty on the accuracy of the information contained herein. This story has not been authorized or endorsed by Corbin Bleu.

In 2005, Corbin Bleu was starring in the TV show Flight
29 Down. He had already acted with some of Hollywood's
biggest stars by the time most fans were introduced to him
in High School Musical.

CHAPTER 1

A Star from the Start

*I*n the dance studio, young Corbin Bleu Reivers was just like any other student. He loved the music, the discipline, and the challenge of mastering new choreography.

Outside the studio, however, the preteen endured endless teasing. Boys, his classmates reasoned, should be playing sports—not learning ballet.

"Twinkle toes." "Fag." "Ballerina boy." The name-calling was merciless, but Reivers ignored it and stayed true to his passion. He told himself his classmates just didn't understand how athletic dance really was, or maybe they were jealous.

"Besides," he says, "my argument was that I got to be surrounded by beautiful girls all day."

These days, those taunting classmates are probably wishing they'd kept quiet. His dance skills, after all, helped propel Reivers—now known simply as Corbin Bleu—to success. Thanks largely to his role in The Disney Channel's

High School Musical movies, he has become a teen sensation. But Bleu's career didn't start with his role in *High School Musical*, and judging from fan reaction to his every move, his star will continue to shine for years to come.

Born February 21, 1989, in Brooklyn, New York, Bleu is the oldest of four children. His parents, David and Martha, met at New York's acclaimed High School of Performing Arts. David Reivers has become a veteran actor, appearing

Corbin Bleu is following in the footsteps of his actor father, David Reivers. The two have done some acting projects together.

in TV shows such as *Charmed, Drake & Josh*, and *My Name Is Earl*.

Bleu was just two years old when he began to follow in his father's footsteps. His warm smile and brown curls helped him win roles in commercials for products including Life cereal, Bounty paper towels, Hasbro toys and games, and Nabisco crackers and cookies. He appeared in print advertisements for stores such as Macy's, Gap, Target, and Toys R Us, and in fashion features in *Child, Parent,* and *American Baby* magazines.

At age four — when most children are learning to print their first names — Bleu signed on with the Ford Modeling Agency in New York. He continued to get jobs modeling for major clients, and within two years he landed his first professional theater role in an off-Broadway production of Barbara Lebow's play, *Tiny Tim Is Dead.* His part, as a homeless, mute child, was a small one, but it sparked his desire to do even more acting.

Bleu and his family moved to Los Angeles in 1996, and he quickly landed a recurring role on . . . High Incident.

Bleu and his family moved to Los Angeles in 1996, and Corbin quickly landed a recurring role on the TV police drama *High Incident*. A steady stream of acting jobs followed. He landed small roles in movies including *Soldier, Mystery Men,* and *Galaxy Quest* and guest-starred on television shows such as *ER, Malcolm & Eddie,* and *The Amanda Show*. Before he was ten years old, he had already

Corbin Bleu starred as Nathan in the Discovery Kids TV series **Flight 29 Down.** *The show told the stories of seven teenage survivors of a plane crash as they worried about setting up camp, finding food and water, and establishing contact with the outside world.*

performed with some of Hollywood's biggest stars: Kurt Russell, Ben Stiller, William H. Macy, Greg Kinnear, Tim Allen, Sigourney Weaver, and George Clooney.

Many young performers might have let this early success go to their head, but Bleu knew he still had a lot to learn. He continued dancing and enrolled as one of the first students at the prestigious Debbie Allen Dance Academy. He later attended the Los Angeles County High School for the Arts as a theater major.

At age sixteen, he was a full-time actor on the brink of becoming a full-fledged star.

It was during his freshman year of high school that Bleu won his first leading role in a feature film, portraying one of three young friends who rob a bank in *Catch That Kid.* Back in classes the next year, he earned parts in the school's productions of *Footloose* and *Grease.* At the end of his sophomore year, he was honored with the award of Theatre Student of the Year. A couple of months later, he became part of the ensemble cast for the Discovery Kids TV series *Flight 29 Down,* filmed on location in Hawaii.

Finally, bouncing between classes and school productions and professional movie sets became too difficult. Bleu left school and earned his high school diploma through homeschooling. At age sixteen, he was a full-time actor on the brink of becoming a full-fledged star.

On his way to Sunday in the Valley, a benefit for A New Leash on Life animal charity, Bleu shows some love to a dog rescued from the 2005 New Orleans floods. A dog lover, he enjoys using his star power to help worthy causes, including a number of organizations that benefit animals.

From Unknown to Megastar

*A*s soon as he read the script for *High School Musical,* Bleu knew he wanted to be a part of it. Getting the part, though, took some real work.

Bleu set out to audition for the role of Ryan, Sharpay's song-and-dance-loving brother. That part ultimately went to Lucas Grabeel.

"I couldn't shake my hips as well as Lucas could," Bleu told *Scholastic News.* Casting directors instead asked him to audition for the part of Troy's basketball-playing best friend, Chad Danforth.

"They brought me in once, then they brought me in for a callback and I really made them laugh," he told *Discovery Girls.* "At that point they said, 'You're good, but we really need to see if you can sing.' And then they brought me in again and said, 'But we need to see if you can dance.' And then they said, 'OK, you're great, but we need to see if you can play basketball.' And then they said, 'We need you to meet the director.'

"It was a long, long process, which originally started with me trying out for a different role," he said. "I've learned, though, that the parts you get are the ones you were meant to get."

Bleu and the rest of the *High School Musical* cast spent a couple of weeks rehearsing before any filming could begin. On location in Salt Lake City and Ogden, Utah, the cast worked from 6:00 A.M. to 6:00 P.M. to improve their singing, dancing, acting, and basketball skills.

The long hours and hard work were worth it. More than 7.7 million viewers watched *High School Musical*'s premiere

High School Musical *cast members, left to right, Lucas Grabeel, Monique Coleman, Corbin Bleu, Ashley Tisdale, Zac Efron, and Vanessa Hudgens, scored at the 2006 Teen Choice Awards. The cast picked up the award for Best TV Show, Comedy/Musical.*

on January 20, 2006. The made-for-TV movie was the number one movie of the month for all basic cable networks. And that was just the beginning. During the next three weeks, 26.3 million unduplicated viewers (meaning even if you watched three different times, you were counted as one viewer) tuned in to watch the teenage love story.

The movie has since been seen by more than 250 million viewers worldwide. It has won two Emmy Awards, a Director's Guild of America Award, the Television Critics Association Award for Outstanding Children's Program, and an Imagen Award for Best Children's Program, among others.

> "High School Musical *is fun. Lots of fun. Sure, other Disney Channel movies have been fun, too, but this one, well, it's downright electric.*"

TV critics, who are not known for generous compliments, overwhelmingly praised *High School Musical.* The *Orlando Sentinel*'s Hal Boedeker, for example, applauded the performers for meeting "their challenges with the same panache that Judy Garland and Mickey Rooney used to display in their MGM musicals." David Cornelius of *DVD Talk* wrote: "*High School Musical* is fun. Lots of fun. Sure, other Disney Channel movies have been fun, too, but this one, well, it's downright electric."

Suddenly the cast of virtual unknowns shot to superstardom—at least among teen, tween, and younger fans. Posters, T-shirts, school supplies, and other merchandise featuring the young actors' images became hot

High School Musical *costars Zac Efron, Vanessa Hudgens, Ashley Tisdale, and Corbin Bleu picked up awards for Best Children's Programming in the Creative Arts category of the 2006 Primetime Emmy Awards. The movie also won an Emmy for Best Choreography.*

sellers. Virtually overnight, Bleu and his costars went from not even being invited to awards shows to being nominees and presenters. They were hounded for autographs and followed by photographers.

Bleu suspects that much of *High School Musical's* success may have come from the fact that there were no preconceived notions about how it might turn out. "We weren't expecting it to be this huge thing," he told the *San Francisco Chronicle.* "We just wanted to go in and create a good movie and somehow caught lightning in a bottle."

Bleu had been an experienced young actor, but the Disney network musical came along and catapulted him to celebrity, showcasing his singing and dancing skills. "It's changed my life in many ways," he said.

From Small Screen to Big Time

*H*igh School Musical helped Bleu amass an enormous following—very quickly. It also launched him from ensemble player to leading-man status.

Jump In!, a made-for-TV Disney movie, features Bleu as Izzy Daniels, a teenage boxing hopeful who finds happiness on a competitive double Dutch team. The movie also stars Keke Palmer *(Akeelah and the Bee)* as Mary, Izzy's friend and fellow jumper.

Bleu trained long and hard for *Jump In!* His daily regimen consisted of two hours of boxing and three hours of double Dutch jump roping. "I trained for two months, boxing and [jumping] double Dutch every single day," he told the *Albany [N.Y.] Times Union.* "Before the movie I stopped working out for a little bit. After the first day of going into that boxing gym, I was falling down."

He picked up the jump rope tricks pretty quickly and thinks his dance background probably helped with that. "It's all about listening to the rope and the rhythm," he told the *Ventura [California] County Star.* "You should be able to do double Dutch with your eyes closed."

Once filming began, he was good enough to perform many of the tricks—like donkey kicks and pushups—himself. But he did have a stunt double for some of the more difficult moves, like backflips.

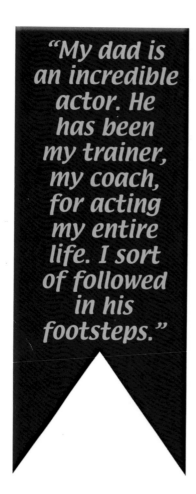

"My dad is an incredible actor. He has been my trainer, my coach, for acting my entire life. I sort of followed in his footsteps."

The movie was especially gratifying for Bleu because his real-life dad, veteran actor David Reivers, portrays Izzy's dad in the film.

"That was one of the best experiences of my entire career," Bleu said. "My dad is an incredible actor. He has been my trainer, my coach, for acting my entire life. I sort of followed in his footsteps."

You might think it would be strange to work with your father, but Bleu says the two were merely coworkers when they were on the set.

"That is one of the most wonderful things about the job: Both of us are about the work and we're very professional," Bleu told the *Times Union.* "When we go on the set, we are two actors working together."

Viewers clearly appreciated Bleu's efforts. When it premiered in January 2007, *Jump In!* broke the record previously set by *The Cheetah Girls 2* as the highest-rated Disney Channel original movie premiere, with 8.2 million viewers.

Corbin Bleu hams it up with actor Zac Efron on the set of NBC's The Today Show. *The young actors found themselves in high demand following the success of 2006's* High School Musical.

Of course, *Jump In!* was later beat out in the ratings race by another film in which Bleu starred: *High School Musical 2*.

HSM2 caught up with the gang on their last day of school and followed them to their summer jobs at a country club. Bleu's character, Chad, toils in the kitchen, while Troy (Zac Efron) works in the golf shop, Gabriella (Vanessa Anne Hudgens) works as a lifeguard, and members Sharpay (Ashley Tisdale) and Ryan (Lucas Grabeel) lounge by the pool. As they endure their own on-the-job challenges, they also face off over the country club's annual midsummer night's musical production.

The Disney film built on the success of its predecessor: 17.2 million viewers tuned in when *High School Musical 2* premiered on August 17, 2007. Those ratings made it the most-watched event to date broadcast on basic cable, surpassing the debut of *Monday Night Football* on ESPN in September 2006. It also became the most-watched movie to be shown on basic cable, smashing the previous record holder, the TNT western *Crossfire Trail,* which was seen by 15.5 million viewers when it aired in January 2001.

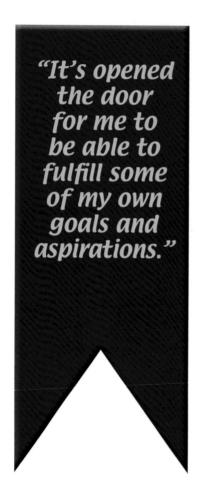

"It's opened the door for me to be able to fulfill some of my own goals and aspirations."

The third installment in the *High School Musical* series would be released in movie theaters in October 2008. The movie follows Troy, Chad, and the gang as they struggle with the idea of being separated from one another as college approaches. Bleu says he's glad for the opportunity to be part of the *High School Musical* franchise, and he believes the third movie will help bring closure for the cast and fans.

"It's been incredible," Bleu told *TheHollywoodGossip.com.* "I have made the most wonderful friends and I've gotten so much exposure. It's opened the door for me to be able to fulfill some of my own goals and aspirations."

CHAPTER 4

In Tune, On Tour

*B*leu grew up singing and playing the piano for his family, but it wasn't until he recorded "Circles in My Mind" for *Flight 29 Down* that he took his talents to a broader audience. That song was just a preview of the musical opportunities that lay ahead.

Music is key to the popularity of the *High School Musical* movies. Fans quickly learned the words to songs and mimicked the cast's dance moves. The sound track from the first *High School Musical* movie shocked everyone when it became the number one album of 2006, outselling popular artists such as Rascal Flatts, Carrie Underwood, Nickelback, Justin Timberlake, and Beyoncé.

That success led to a two-month, 40-city *High School Musical* concert tour in 2007. The concert featured Bleu along with cast members Ashley Tisdale and Vanessa Hudgens. Drew Seeley, who cowrote "Get'cha Head in the Game" and sang on the *High School Musical* sound track, also sang in the concerts.

High School Musical *cast members dazzled audiences in arenas around the world. Their 40-city concert tour featured songs from the original production and also showcased some of the film's main actors, who were promoting albums of their own.*

The tour was Bleu's first chance to perform in front of cheering fans. "It was really, really fun," he told the *Detroit Free Press.*

He also admitted that the concert tour experience was both exhausting and exhilarating. "Throughout the day of the show, all of us were groggy," he told *Discoverygirls.com.* "And then, once the audience started to arrive and we'd hear them, we'd start getting pumped. Once onstage, we were all crazy. But after the show, we'd still have that energy and then we'd have to travel to the next city. It took us until about three in the morning to get there, and we usually just stayed up until then."

Bleu says there are enormous differences between filming a movie and being part of a live concert tour. "Being onstage is all about keeping it fresh every night and it's about the energy and your connection between the audience and the people onstage with you," he said. "The film is a start-and-stop thing. You have to be in your head a lot more and really get into character. Onstage for a concert, it's all about getting up every single last bit of energy to give to that audience. When you have an audience of 15,000 screaming people watching you, it's not that hard to get that energy going."

In *Jump In!*, Bleu sang "Push It to the Limit," the lead song on the movie's sound track. The single quickly became number one on Radio Disney and entered Billboard's Hot 100 chart at number 14.

Despite his busy acting and touring schedule, Bleu found time to record his first solo album. *Another Side* was released by Hollywood Records on May 1, 2007. The album was released after *Jump In!* debuted but before *High School Musical 2* did. The album, which Bleu calls "pop-R&B," features *High School Musical* costar Vanessa Anne Hudgens on the track "Still There for Me." *Another Side* debuted at number 36 on the U.S. Billboard 200, selling about 18,000 copies in its first week.

> "Onstage for a concert, it's all about getting up every single last bit of energy to give to that audience."

Bleu cowrote five of the songs on his first album but says he still "freaks out" when he hears his voice on the radio. "I'm self-conscious about it," he told *CosmoGirl!* "But people say it's a different kind of sound they can't exactly pinpoint, which is cool."

Although touring can be exhausting, Bleu loves performing live.

In support of his first album, Bleu joined up with teen pop stars Aly & AJ and Drake Bell to headline NextFest, a tour that hit 29 cities in summer 2007. That tour coincided with the premiere of *High School Musical 2*. The movie sound track—featuring Bleu singing "What Time Is It? (Summertime!)," "I Don't Dance," "Everyday," "All for One," and "Work This Out"—debuted at number 1 on the U.S. Billboard 200. The sound track sold 615,000 copies in its initial week of release. By the end of 2007, it had sold more than 5 million copies worldwide.

At work on his second album in early 2008, Bleu said he plans to do more writing for his sophomore effort but he has other, long-range musical plans as well. "I want to be on Broadway so bad," he said. "And I want to direct eventually."

Graduating from High School

*B*leu is the first to admit that show business isn't easy, but it is his passion. "The job is not steady. You never know when you're going to work," he told *TheStarScoop.com*. "You have to go a whole year or two and nothing comes in. A lot of times they're not looking for your type, especially because I'm mixed." (He is of Italian and Jamaican descent.) "A lot of times they either want to go full on Caucasian or they want to go full on black. They either want somebody who is really black and from the street and urban and a little bit ghetto or they want a Caucasian. That's probably one of the hardest struggles for me. You never know when work is going to come."

You might think that because Bleu started out in the business as a toddler, he's getting bored with it. The truth is, over the years, his love for acting has grown. He's proud of his dedication to the craft and tries to learn something about it from every project and experience.

The NAACP Image Awards honor projects and individuals that promote diversity in the arts of television, recording, literature, and motion pictures. In 2008, Bleu was nominated for Outstanding New [Recording] Artist. High School Musical 2 was nominated for Outstanding Children's Program.

"For me, it's not all about the fame and fortune; it's really [about] putting out good work," he said.

While many young celebrities have made headlines for their bad behavior and bad decisions, Bleu is proud to stay grounded. He credits his parents for providing him with love, support, and lots of great advice. "I have really great parents who have constantly kept me grounded my whole life," he said. Explaining how he avoids becoming "a robot," he added, "You have to remember that [acting] is a job; it's not [about changing into] this whole other entity that they try to make it all about [when you become] a celebrity. Remember there are people struggling in this world, and you're just lucky enough to be able to get what you have. Stay humble, and remember that [being a celebrity is] your job. Accept it graciously, and don't make a big deal of it."

Bleu walks the talk, using his star power to help promote worthwhile causes and events. The actor is an ambassador for the Starlight Starbright Children's Foundation, an organization dedicated to helping seriously ill children and their families cope with their fear, pain and isolation. Among his other causes: Make-A-Wish Foundation, a wish-granting organization for terminally ill children, and Artists for a New South Africa, a group working in the United States and South Africa to fight HIV/AIDS.

> "Remember there are people struggling in this world, and you're just lucky enough to be able to get what you have."

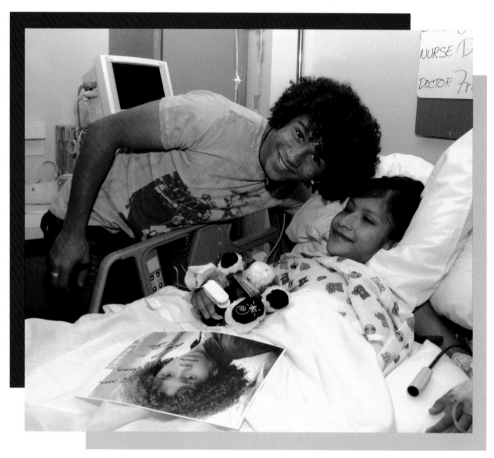

Bleu visits a young fan at Shriners Hospital for Children in Los Angeles in 2007. He has made it a priority to give his time, energy, and money to organizations that benefit children and animals.

Bleu is grateful for the boost *High School Musical* has given his career, but once the third movie is released, he's hoping for a different kind of role to really prove his acting chops. Recognizing that he's a hot commodity—at least for the moment—Bleu is taking time to review the many scripts he's being sent. He's careful to choose those that are best for him. First up: *Free Style,* a movie Bleu is both producing and starring in. It also features his father David Reivers, Madison Pettis (from Disney Channel's *Cory in the House*), and Penelope Ann Miller (from *Blonde Ambition, The Messengers*).

Free Style stars Bleu as a young man who is devoted to his family. He finds love and himself in his quest to win the Amateur National Motocross Championship. It's a bit grittier than *High School Musical,* but not so gritty that fans will be shocked.

"I think it's time to take it to another level," he told *EW.com.* "It's always fun to have a challenge; something that makes it a little more of a transition into being an adult. Not that I would want to, you know, go completely over the top and be very risky and risqué, because I would never want to lose the core audience that I have right now. It's about continuing to grow up like I have naturally."

One dream Bleu has is to someday appear on the big screen along with some of his favorite actors, like Johnny Depp or Meryl Streep.

"Just working with people that are truly legends and who have been through it—that rubs off. You learn from them," he told *EW.com.* "I'd like to play a few roles, and then go do another album, and then go work on Broadway. I love change. I love trying new things."

And his fans love that about him.

> *"I'd like to play a few roles, and then go do another album, and then go work on Broadway. I love change. I love trying new things."*

1989 Corbin Bleu Reivers is born February 21 in Brooklyn, New York.

1991 He begins appearing in TV commercials.

1993 He signs with the Ford Modeling Agency.

1995 Corbin appears in his first professional theater production, *Tiny Tim Is Dead.*

1996 Corbin's family moves to Los Angeles, and Corbin lands a recurring role on the TV series *High Incident.*

2004 He joins Los Angeles County High School for the Performing Arts. He is cast in his first leading role in the feature film *Catch That Kid.* He becomes part of the ensemble cast of *Flight 29 Down.*

2005 He earns his high school diploma. He is cast as Chad Danforth in *High School Musical.*

2006 *High School Musical* airs January 20. It becomes Disney Channel's most successful movie at the time, with 7.7 million viewers for its first U.S. broadcast. Corbin signs on as a StarPower Ambassador with Starlight Starbright Children's Foundation, an organization dedicated to helping seriously ill children and their families.

2007 *Jump In!* is released. Corbin releases his album *Another Side.* *High School Musical 2* premieres August 17 to 17.2 million viewers, making it the most-watched event ever broadcast on basic cable.

2008 Filming begins on *High School Musical 3: Senior Year;* Corbin teams up with Sara Lee to promote nutritious school lunches. *Free Style* is scheduled for release. He begins working on his second album.

FILMOGRAPHY

Theatrical Releases

2008 *Free Style*

High School Musical 3

2004 *Catch That Kid*

1999 *Family Tree*

Mystery Men

Galaxy Quest

1998 *Soldier*

Television

2007 *Jump In!*

High School Musical 2

2006 *High School Musical*

2005–2007 *Flight 29 Down*

DISCOGRAPHY

Albums

2007 *Another Side*

Sound Track Contributions

2008 "Run It Back Again" on *Radio Disney Jams, Vol. 10*

2007 *Jump In!*

High School Musical 2 Sound Track

2006 *High School Musical Sound Track*

Books

Scott, Dee. *Corbin Bleu: Up Close.* New York: Pocket Books, 2006.

West, Betsy. *Corbin Bleu to the Limit: An Unauthorized Biography.* New York: Price Stern Sloan, 2007.

Works Consulted

Alexander, George. "NAACP Image Award Nominations." *Black Enterprise,* http://www.blackenterprise.com/cms/exclusivesopen.aspx?id=4028

Campbell, Janis. "*High School Musical 2:* Yakking with Vanessa and Corbin." *Detroit Free Press,* July 31, 2007, page 4E.

Chang, Rachel. "Corbin Bleu at 10 a.m." *CosmoGirl!,* February 2007, page 22.

"Corbin Bleu." *The Star Scoop,* n.d., www.thestarscoop.com/archives/corbin-bleu.php

"Corbin Bleu, Monique Coleman Speak on *High School Musical.*" *The Hollywood Gossip,* August 23, 2007, www.thehollywoodgossip.com/2007/08/corbin-bleu-monique-coleman-speak-on-high-school-musical

"Getting to Know Corbin Bleu." *Teen,* http://www.teenmag.com/celeb-stuff/corbin-bleu

Gonzalez, Maria Cortes. "Corbin Bleu Finds Himself in Full Whirlwind Tour Mode." *El Paso Times,* July 12, 2007.

"*Jump In*'s Corbin Bleu." *People Weekly,* February 5, 2007, page 130.

Kirsten, Naomi. "Catching Up with Corbin Bleu." n.d., http://www.discoverygirls.com/entertainment/celebrities/catching-corbin-bleu

McGuire, Mark. "Disney's Corbin Bleu Graduates from 'High School.'" [Albany, N.Y.] *Times Union,* January 12, 2007, page D1.

Mason, Dave. "Corbin Bleu Stars in Latest Disney Channel TV Movie." *Ventura [California] County Star*, January 12, 2007.

Miller, Gerri. "Catching Up with the Cast of *High School Musical*." *Scholastic News*, n.d., http://teacher.scholastic.com/scholasticnews/indepth/highschoolmusical2.asp

Mitovich, Matt Webb. "*High School Musical*'s Corbin Bleu Hits the Ropes." *TV Guide*, January 12, 2007.

Rizzo, Carita. "Corbin Bleu Ponders the Pressures on 'High School Musical' Stars." *TV Guide*, October 9, 2007.

Shepherd, Julianne. "Corbin Bleu: The Renaissance Boy." *Vibe*, September 2007.

Soll, Lindsay. " 'Musical' Revival?" EW.com, http://www.ew.com/ew/article/0,,20052967,00.html.

Southern, Nathan. "Corbin Bleu Biography," *All Movie Guide*, on Starpulse.com, http://www.starpulse.com/Actors/Bleu,_Corbin/Biography/

Tsai, Michael. " 'Flight 29'-ers Shake Stardust, Walk On." *Honolulu Advertiser*, February 17, 2006.

Vaziri, Aidin. "Pop Quiz: Corbin Bleu." *San Francisco Chronicle*, April 1, 2007, page 44, *Sunday Datebook*.

On the Internet

Corbin Bleu — Official Site
   http://www.corbinbleu.com

High School Musical On Tour
   http://disney.go.com/theatre/highschoolmusical/

INDEX